C000156031

100 FACTS, MYTHS & LEGENDS ABOUT GLOUCESTER

Matt Cass & Paul James

Copyright © 2021 Matt Cass & Paul James

All rights reserved

The characters and events portrayed in this book are
fictitious. Any similarity to real persons, living or dead, is
coincidental and not intended by the author.

No part of this book may be reproduced, or stored in a
retrieval system, or transmitted in any form or by any
means, electronic, mechanical, photocopying, recording,
or otherwise, without express written permission of the
publisher.

ISBN-13: 9798777021229
ISBN-10: 1477123456

Cover design by: Art Painter
Library of Congress Control Number: 2018675309
Printed in the United States of America

This book is dedicated to the City of Gloucester and to all the interesting Characters, Facts, Myths and Stories that make it such a special place; without them we could not have written this book.

Thanks also to our wives and families who have helped, questioned and challenged us and made their own suggestions (polite and otherwise!) while we have been compiling this book

CONTENTS

INTRODUCTION

Gloucester is a fascinating place. Centuries ago it was one of the most important cities in England. With 2000 years of history, you'd expect a few interesting things to have happened along the way. But even in the 21st century history is still being made here.

Researching the people, places and stories that make up this book has been a real pleasure. The biggest challenge was limiting it to only 100 items!

We hope it helps people from the city and beyond to appreciate what a rich heritage, both ancient and modern, there is in Gloucester and encourages as many people as possible to explore what it has to offer.

We hope you enjoy reading it as much as we've enjoyed writing it

SYNOPSIS

Did you know that the nursery rhyme Humpty Dumpty is claimed to owe its origins to Gloucester during the English Civil War? Or that a poem written by a Gloucestrian kept Nelson Mandela's spirits up whilst he was incarcerated for 27 years? Or that the very same poet was the inspiration for Long John Silver in Treasure Island? Had you realised that Gloucester Cathedral was once destined for demolition or that The Beatles played in what is now a Wetherspoons pub or that the vacuum cleaner was invented right here in Gloucester?

All these stories, facts, rumours, myths and more are collated for the first time in this book.

PEOPLE

The Inspiration for Long John Silver and the Poem that Sustained Mandela.

William Ernest Henley was born in Eastgate Street, Gloucester in 1849 and attended The Crypt School. He is most famous for his poem, 'Invictus', which was read each day by **Nelson Mandela** when he was incarcerated for 27 years. It was also the inspiration for the 2009 film 'Invictus', **starring Morgan Freeman and Matt Damon**, about South Africa winning the 1995 Rugby World Cup. Henley, who had a leg amputated due to tuberculosis, was also believed to be the inspiration for **Long John Silver** in his friend Robert Louis Stevenson's book 'Treasure Island'.

The Second Signatory to the US Declaration of Independence

Button Gwinnett, second signatory to the US Declaration of Independence, was born at Down Hatherley, just outside Gloucester in 1735. His father was vicar of Down Hatherley Church and also of St Nicholas' Church in Westgate Street. For a while they rented a house in College Green, by the Cathedral. Button moved to Georgia where he became Governor. He died after being shot in the leg by his long-time rival Lachlan McIntosh. Due to its rarity his signature is **highly valuable with one selling for $722,500 at auction**. He is also a character in the popular **computer game Fallout 3**.

The Inventor of the Vacuum Cleaner

Hubert Cecil Booth, inventor of the vacuum cleaner, was born at Theresa Place in Gloucester (now part of Bristol Road by the Linden Tree pub). He lived at Park House, Spa Road as a young boy (a blue plaque there marks the fact). He invented the first powered vacuum cleaner, a large machine which was nick-named the **'Puffing Billy'**. It was used to clean the carpets of Westminster Abbey prior to Edward VII's coronation in 1901. He also designed **ferris wheels, bridges and factories**.

Gloucester Born (But Not Bred)

A number of high-profile figures have been born in Gloucester, although they didn't live here. These include the Government's Chief Medical Officer **Professor Chris Whitty**, former England cricket captain **Alastair Cook** and BBC Breakfast television presenter **Charlie Stayt**.

The Boy Band Member from a Girl's School

Nathan Sykes, of boy band **The Wanted**, grew up in Gloucester and attended Ribston Hall High School Sixth Form. For a while he was dating American pop star Ariana Grande. The Wanted formed in 2009 until 2014 and had a reunion in 2020.

The Inspiration for Ebenezer Scrooge

Jemmy Wood (1756-1838) ran the Gloucester Old Bank in Westgate Street (now McDonalds). He became known nationally as the **"Gloucester Miser"** and appeared in statuettes, cartoons and Toby Jugs. He is believed to have been the inspiration for Dickens' character **Ebenezer Scrooge in 'A Christmas Carol'**. His wealth of around £900,000 **made him the richest commoner in England**, but most of the money he left in his will was used up on lawyers' fees because of a dispute amongst beneficiaries. This may have inspired Dickens to write about the case of Jarndyce v Jarndyce in his novel "Bleak House".

Jemmy Wood

Sailed from Gloucester to Gloucester

Captain Howard Blackburn (1859-1932) was a Canadian-American fisherman, who lost his fingers and toes to frostbite while lost at sea. Despite this, he single-handedly sailed across the Atlantic from Gloucester Massachusetts to Gloucester, England in 1899, being at sea for 62 days. He arrived at Sharpness in his 30-foot vessel Great Western and was towed along the canal by the SS Sabrina into Gloucester Docks, where a spectacular reception awaited.

The Question Time Presenter

Former Question Time presenter, the late **Sir Robin Day** briefly attended The Crypt School in Gloucester. His father was a telephone engineer who became telephone manager at Gloucester. In his autobiography, 'Grand Inquisitor' Sir Robin admitted to being caned on his 10th birthday by Crypt headmaster D. G. Williams for being noisy and disorderly in morning assembly!

The Man in Charge of Westminster Abbey

David Hoyle, who was a Canon at Gloucester Cathedral, was appointed Dean of Westminster Abbey in 2019 - which means he is likely to be called upon to officiate at any major royal occasions at the Abbey during his period of office. He still has family in Gloucester.

Thatcher's Cabinet Minister

Peter Walker was one of the longest-serving Cabinet Ministers of the 20th century, serving in Edward Heath's and Margaret Thatcher's Cabinets. He was also a co-founder of the Slater Walker bank which later had to be bailed out by the Bank of England in the 1970s. He began his political life as Chairman of Gloucester Young Conservatives and started his business career at the General Accident insurance office in Brunswick Road. He was the world's first Environment Minister and, in that role, he officially opened the newly-developed Kings Square in May 1972.

The Inventor of the Wheatstone Bridge

Barnwood-born **Charles Wheatstone** was a serial inventor responsible for the electro-telegraph, electric clock, code transmitter and **the Wheatstone Bridge**, used to measure electrical resistance to this day by physicists. He also invented numerous versions of the concertina. Sadly, his wind piano and bellows violin didn't catch on.

Gloucester's Record-Breaking Superhero

In 2012, Gloucester resident **Jamie McDonald** decided to **cycle 14,000 miles from Bangkok to his hometown**, passing through dozens of countries. Along the way he was shot at, arrested and slept rough. Just two days after he came back, he decided to attempt the **world static non-stop cycling record**, which stood at 224 hours and 24 minutes. Pushing through sleep deprivation (and an infected backside!), he kept pedalling for a world-record breaking 268 hours.

In February 2014, Jamie became the first person in history to **run the 5,000 miles (200 marathons)** across Canada from the Atlantic coast to the Pacific coast without the aid of a support crew. He battled -40°C temperatures, a frostbitten nose, and numerous potentially challenge-stopping injuries.

In 2018 **he ran 5,500 miles across America**, finishing in Gloucester, Massachusetts, raising nearly $200,000 for sick children. Just weeks later, he broke another endurance **world record, running 524 miles over 7 days on a treadmill.** Jamie, known as Adventureman, has established the Superhero Foundation to support families' fundraising effort.

Jamie McDonald

The World's Loudest Town Crier

Gloucester's Town Crier Alan Myatt set two Guinness World Records. As well as being the loudest crier, recording a cry of 112.8 decibels, he also set the Guinness world record for vocal endurance, issuing a one hundred word proclamation every 15 minutes for a period of 48 hours.

Alan Myatt

The First Woman Bishop

Rachel Treweek was appointed **Bishop of Glouces-ter** in June 2015 and became **the first women Dio-cesan Bishop in the country**. She was also **the first woman Bishop to sit in the House of Lords** as a Lord Spiritual.

Her appointment as Bishop of Gloucester **was seen as an important signal about women holding key positions of power and influence. Soon after she took up her position**, the roles of Lord Lieutenant, High Sheriff, Chief Constable and Bishop in Glouces-tershire **were all held by women.**

Stunt Man's 18 World Records

Gloucester daredevil stunt driver **Dick Sheppard** (1931-2021) appeared in every edition of the Guin-ness Book of Records from 1969 to 1996. He boasted that he had wrecked 2,003 cars, appeared in 500 films including the iconic **'Italian Job,'** and held **18 world records** during his career. Dick's first world record - one of his favourites - was in 1969 when he rode an ex-army motorbike through a 100 foot tunnel of fire. He regarded it as a record that will never be beaten because after four people had died trying it was withdrawn from the Guinness Book of Records.

The Seagull Victim who Became an International Celebrity

Gloucester car park boss **Don Weston**, who died in 2019, shot to worldwide fame while he suffered regular attacks every summer from a **seagull dubbed the "Wellington Bomber"**. Don's experiences with the gull made him such a celebrity that he appeared on **German TV** and was invited to **set the balls rolling for the Italian national lottery**. He also became **well known in Japan.**

The Model who Gloucester Put in the Frame

Page Three girl and model **Melinda Messenger's** career was kickstarted when she took a job modelling for a Gloucester-based double-glazing company, **Glevum Windows**, dressed only in pants and a bra. As part of an advertising campaign called **"Class Behind Glass",** the posters quickly began disappearing from bus stops, having been taken by locals. After a complaint at the lack of clothes on Messenger, the Advertising Standards Authority banned the campaign, claiming they were not sufficiently "classy".

The War Poet

Poet **Ivor Gurney** was born in Gloucester in 1890 in Queen Street (near the Boots store in Eastgate Street). There is a stained glass window in Gloucester Cathedral in his honour by celebrated artist Tom Denny.

The Michelin-Star Winning Celebrity Chef

Michelin-starred celebrity chef and television star **Tom Kerridge** was brought up in Gloucester and attended Saintbridge School. His mother still lives in the city and he regularly comes back to see her and watch Gloucester Rugby at Kingsholm. When asked, he said that **his favourite meal was fish and chips from Danny Dyke's chip shop in Linden**. He has named a spicy accompaniment to his 'posh' fish and chips **'Matson Sauce'** after the Gloucester suburb. Kerridge, who has two Michelin stars, serves a luxury version of the British staple for £32.50 (2019 prices) at his restaurant in the Corinthia Hotel, near Whitehall, central London.

The Hollywood Actor

Actor **Simon Pegg** was born in Brockworth. He is the **award-winning Shaun of the Dead actor.** He is co writer and star of the **"Cornetto Trilogy".** The nickname given to the three movies he wrote with Edgar Wright: **Shaun of the Dead, Hot Fuzz and The World's End**.

He is has also starred in some big Hollywood productions including the **Mission Impossible franchise**, Ice Age and many others. He **plays Scotty in the new Star Trek movies** as well as **starring in the new Star Wars as Unkar Plutt**, one time owner of the Millennium Falcon. He is one of very few actors, if not the only actor, **to star in both Star Wars and Star Trek**.

Simon Pegg

PLACES

The Monks Retreat ... from Wales

Llanthony Priory in Gloucester, or to give it its correct title **Llanthony Secunda Priory**, was founded
in 1136 when the monks of Llanthony Priory in the
Black Mountains in Wales retreated there following attacks from the local population - hence the
'Secunda' (second) part of the name. It was founded
by Miles of Gloucester who was the High Constable
of England who lived at Gloucester Castle (which inspired the name of the local Wetherspoons pub The
Lord High Constable of England). The Priory owned
a huge amount of land, stretching as far as Podsmead, as well as further land in Ireland.

Evacuation of Gloucester ... Almost

During the floods of 2007, **Walham Power Station**
just outside Gloucester was in danger of being en-
gulfed. This would have led to the power to 600,000
homes being lost. A major effort involving the emer-
gency services and the military led to the Power Station being saved. A ring of 'hescobastians' was built
- a collapsible wire mesh container and heavy duty
fabric liner, which is filled with sand, soil or gravel.
The flood water was just two inches below the level
at which the power station would have been en-
gulfed. The media reported at the time that **the au-
thorities were considering evacuating parts of the
County** if that had happened.

The Battle of Two Kings

Alney Island, to the west of Gloucester, was, possibly, the scene of an important medieval battle. The Anglo-Saxon Chronicle records that Cnut, the Danish king, fought and defeated the English king Edmund Ironside there in 1016.

Street Name Change Proposal didn't have a Monopoly on Good Ideas

Cromwell Street in Gloucester was almost renamed **'Park Lane'** in the aftermath of the Fred and Rose West murder discoveries, but the suggestion was rejected by residents. Goodness knows what the well-heeled residents of the upmarket London street of the same name, which appears on the Monopoly Board, would have made of it!

The Longest Unbroken Railway Station Platform

At 1,977 feet 4 inches (602.69 m), **Gloucester Railway Station** has the second-longest platform in the UK - the longest is Colchester's platform at 2034 ft (620 m), albeit Gloucester has the longest unbroken platform, as Colchester's is two different physical platforms.

It 'Asda' be an Old Railway Station

The Asda supermarket in Bruton Way is on the site of the former **Gloucester Eastgate railway station**. There were three platforms and a footbridge linked it to the current Gloucester Central station. It closed in 1975.

Kylie's Ancestor wasn't so Lucky

Kylie and Dannii Minogue's great-great-great-great-great-grandmother, 69-year-old **Dinah Riddiford** and her son Luke were jailed in Gloucester for stealing two sides of bacon, two pigs' cheeks, one piece of tongue, a large pat of butter in an earthenware pot and a small copper tea kettle. Dinah was sent to the prison roof on 7th September 1816 for a public execution which became known in Gloucestershire as **"The Granny Hanging",** while Luke was sent down under to the penal colonies in Australia.

Within the main Victorian block at Gloucester prison, you can see serpent-shaped brackets lining the walls. These are symbolic and said to represent evil. Closer examination reveals a lion's claw at the base of the railing above the serpent, symbolising justice bearing down on the evil.

The site of the Prison **was previously Gloucester Castle**. It was first documented **in the Domesday book**, where it is recorded that sixteen houses were demolished to make way for it. It became a Royal Castle in 1155. Henry III often stayed there and in 1214 King John's wife, Queen Isabella, was imprisoned there until her death in 1216.

Cathedral almost Demolished

The Great East Window at **Gloucester Cathedral** boasted the accolade of being **the largest window in the world** when it was installed in the 1350s, and still remains a landmark of English and European medieval stained glass. Reaching 22-metres high and 12-metres wide, the window is as big as a tennis court. The window was created as part of the reconstruction of the Quire following the burial of King Edward II. **It was carefully dismantled during the Second World War** and kept in the Crypt of the Cathedral to keep it safe, then put back together when the war was over.

Under **Oliver Cromwell**, Gloucester Cathedral was not only neglected but **in danger of demolition**. Between 1652-1657 a syndicate was formed with the objective of pulling the building down. It was only by obtaining a transfer to themselves that the Mayor and Corporation were able to save it from destruction.

In 2016 Gloucester Cathedral joined the campaign to reduce the Church of England's carbon emissions. In order to help reach their target Gloucester Cathedral commissioned installation of solar panels on the cathedral roof. The installation made the 1,000-year-old building **the oldest Cathedral in the UK with a solar installation.** The panels were blessed on the BBC regional television news by the Dean of Gloucester, the Very Reverend Stephen Lake.

Fortress Kingsholm

Roman Gloucester itself began life as a fortress at Kingsholm. **Kingsholm** later became the site of a Saxon royal palace (Kynge's Holme) used during the reign of Edward the Confessor as a meeting place for the Great Council. The area around Kingsholm was used as a Roman burial ground.

The Furthest Inland Port

Gloucester is said to be the furthest inland port in the UK, although Goole in East Yorkshire also makes the same claim. Gloucester was given the formal status of a port by letters patent from **Queen Elizabeth I i**n 1580.

This meant that vessels could trade directly between Gloucester and foreign ports without having to call in at Bristol custom house, which had previously been responsible for the area. Gloucester Corporation hoped to benefit from the new status because they collected dues on goods handled at Gloucester's riverside Quay. In practice, however, few foreign-going vessels were seen at the Quay because of the difficulties of navigating the shallow tidal stretch of the River Severn approaching the city.

The Best-Preserved Dominican Friary in the Country

Built in 1239, Gloucester's **Blackfriars Priory**, which is **the best-preserved Dominican friary in the country**, stands on the bailey of William the Conqueror's castle. After Henry VIII dissolved the monasteries in the mid-sixteenth century, the site was bought by Sir Thomas Bell who converted the buildings around the cloister into a hat and cloth factory and made his home in the former church. Ladybellegate Street is named after his wife. The Scriptorium on the **south side of the Cloister is the oldest surviving purpose-built library building in Britain.**

Blackfriars Priory

The Car Park Super High-Way

After the city centre development of the 1970s, the **rooftop car parks** at **Eastgate and Kings Walk** and the multi-storey car park at **Longsmith Street** were all linked via bridges over Eastgate Street and Southgate Street - meaning you could easily drive from one to another if you couldn't find a space!

The Building Made from The Wood of The Mayflower?

The **Old Bell Inn** in Southgate Street, where the evangelist **George Whitefield** was born, has a timber facade, which may have been built from the **wood of the Mayflower** - an English ship that transported a group of English families, known today as the Pilgrims, from England to the New World (America) in 1620.

Eastgate Street was once a Jewish Quarter

Eastgate Street once **had its very own Jewish community** which is recorded from 1168 and was one of the most important in Medieval England. The site of their synagogue was opposite St Michael's church, most likely where Thorntons was until recently. In 1217, Henry III confirmed the right of the Jews of Eastgate Street to live in Gloucester. But in 1275, wicked Queen Eleanor revoked that right and expelled the entire Jewish community to Bristol.

The Nightclub with the Steamy Past

The main nightclub in **Eastgate Street**, previously known as Liquid and now Atik, was previously the **city's public baths**. Opening in 1891, there were several swimming pools, a Turkish bath, steam rooms and 'slipper baths' where men working at the foundry and on the railway would come after work and bathe before going home.

The Old Public Baths

HISTORY

Gloucester was Founded by a Roman Emperor

Gloucester was most probably founded in the reign of the **Emperor Nerva (96-98 AD),** for the Roman town was named after him: Colonia Nerviana Glevensis. A colonia was a settlement of retired army veterans.

To celebrate the 1900th anniversary of the foundation of Gloucester, in 2002 an equestrian statue of Emperor Nerva by Anthony Stones was erected on the same place where pieces of a bronze equestrian statue were discovered. Nerva was over 60 and rather frail when proclaimed emperor, but the statue shows him as convention dictates: as a military leader. There is also a non-equestrian statue of him in Rome.

Under the plinth is a time capsule containing over 200 items including a signed shirt by **Phil Vickery**, a matching **set of M&S men's and ladies' underwear**, letters from Parmjit Dhanda - MP for Gloucester, and **Pam Tracey** - Mayor of Gloucester and **Harry Potter** DVDs.

Roman Emperor Nerva

Alfred the Great's Daughter who Created England (and inspired Netflix!)

Aethelflaed, Lady of the Mercians, was the daughter of King Alfred the Great and ruled Mercia from 911 until her death in 918. She is **buried at St Oswalds Priory in Gloucester**. In 2018, a re-enactment of her funeral took place in the city to mark the 1100th anniversary of her death.

She is best known for **fighting off the Vikings and uniting kingdoms to create England** as we know it today. She is also responsible for much of the city centre's street pattern. Her story inspired **the Netflix series 'The Last Kingdom'** and the **character Eowyn in Tolkien's 'Lord of The Rings'**.

St Oswalds Priory

The Domesday Book was Ordered Here

The extraordinary historical tome, the **Domesday Book** was planned right here in the city, when **William the Conqueror held the Christmas Court in Gloucester** back in 1085, directing his men to visit shires across England, and to find out how the land was occupied.

A New Queen Hailed at the New Inn

In 1553 King Edward VI died. **Lady Jane Grey was proclaimed Queen** from the steps of the New Inn by the Abbot of Gloucester, a reign that lasted 9 days. Although legend has it she was staying at the New Inn at the time, historians say there is no evidence to support this.

Doctor Foster was Based on King Edward I Coming to Gloucester

The nursery rhyme "**Doctor Foster went to Gloucester**" is believed to be based on a story of **King Edward I** of England travelling to Gloucester, falling off his horse into a puddle, and refusing to return to the city again.

Humpty Dumpty Originated from the Siege of Gloucester

It is claimed that the **Siege of Gloucester** was the origin for the **nursery rhyme Humpty Dumpty**. It was said to be the name of a **large mortar** imported from Holland, mounted on the walls of **Llanthony Secunda Priory** where the Royalist forces were encamped during the Siege. It was apparently named (disparagingly) after a famously rotund MP of the day. As the artillerymen trained their sights on Gloucester's Cathedral, the cannon misfired. Another assertion was that Humpty Dumpty was a 'tortoise' siege engine that featured a series of covered bridges to enable King Charles I's men to cross the defensive ditch and scale the city walls.

The First Christian King Could be Buried Here

A local legend, first recorded in the eighteenth century, states that **St Mary de Lode Church** in Archdeacon Street was the burial place of the legendary **King Lucius, first Christian King of Britain.** This legend combined with the results of archaeological work has apparently inspired the local belief that the church was built on the site of an ancient Roman temple, and was the **first Christian church in Britain.**

There's a King Buried at Gloucester Cathedral (Who Came to a Nasty Ending!)

King Edward II is buried at the Cathedral. Edward was forced to abdicate and was then imprisoned at **Berkeley Castle**, where **he was murdered** on 21 September 1327 (with, as legend would have it, the assistance of **a red-hot poker**).

It was Edward's defeat to Robert the Bruce at the Battle of Bannockburn at 1314 which inspired the song **'Flower of Scotland'** which is frequently performed at special occasions and sporting events as the **official national anthem of Scotland.**

The Tomb of Edward II

William the Conqueror's Son is Buried There Too

Robert, Duke of Normandy, eldest son of William the Conqueror **is also buried at Gloucester Cathedral.** On his death William divided his dominions by giving Robert the Duchy of Normandy and his second son William Rufus the Kingdom of England.

The Tomb of Robert of Normandy

The Boy King Crowned in Gloucester

Gloucester Cathedral (then St Peter's Abbey) hosted the **coronation of King Henry III** in 1216 **when he was just 9 years old**. The royal crown had been either lost or sold during the civil war, so instead the ceremony used a simple gold band. By a strange quirk of fate **the city of his coronation became his prison** when in 1263 Simon de Montfort held him captive in Gloucester Castle during the Barons War.

Henry III Coronation as depicted in a stained glass window in Gloucester Cathedral

The Governor of the Bank of England from Gloucester

Gloucester has several connections with the **Bank of England. Thomas Raikes**, brother of Sunday School founder Robert, was its Governor from 1797 to 1799. **The first Bank of England branch was opened in Northgate Street** (where TK Maxx is now) in 1826. The Registrar's Department of the Bank was based in Southgate House opposite the Docks from 1991-2004.

The Princess, The Baker and The Well...

The inspiration for the **public art piece on Kimbrose Triangle**, known locally as the **CD rack**, is Gloucester's "patron saint" **Kyneburgh,** who, according to medieval legend, was a Saxon princess who ran away from an arranged marriage. She fled to Gloucester and was adopted by a baker whose wife killed her out of jealousy and threw her body down a well. Standing at the bottom of it and looking up makes **you feel like you are at the bottom of a well.**

Nelson's Visit to Gloucester

Horatio Nelson, who defeated Napoleon at the Battle of Trafalgar, stayed at the **Kings Head on Westgate Street** with Lord and Lady Hamilton on 24th July 1802, visited the Cathedral and gifted money to prisoners in Gloucester gaol because he was mindful that many of his crew members were ex-cons.

The Siege of Gloucester Changed the Course of the English Civil War

By 1643 **Gloucester stood alone against the King** in the west of England, and on August 10th a **Royalist army of 30,000 men** led by **Charles** I besieged the city. His opponent was 23 year-old **Lieutenant Colonel Edward Massie** who, as commander of the Gloucester garrison, had just over **1500 men** under him. Despite this, the reinforced Medieval walls of Gloucester **withstood the King's artillery bombardment for 26 days until a relieving Parliamentary army arrived from London**. That day – 5th September 1643 – became known as **Gloucester Day**. Without Gloucester's resistance, the King could have triumphed and Parliament's role would have been diminished.

Massie was later elected Member of Parliament for Gloucester and during the reign of Charles II he was knighted and recommended to be Governor of Jamaica.

Charles II, remembering Gloucester's defiance during the Civil War, gave orders **for the city wall to be demolished.** Sections of it do survive however, mostly below ground, in several locations around Gloucester including in the Museum of Gloucester and the furniture store on the corner of Southgate Street and Parliament Street.

Some people say that the city's modern-day revenge

is that a statue of Charles II, which was previously in the city's long-since demolished Wheat Market in Southgate Street, is now tucked away by some former council flats in St Mary's Square.

It is said that after the Siege of Gloucester, **the Barton area was removed from the city** and so as a response decided to **mock them** and **elect their own mayor, hence the title The Mock Mayor of Barton**. The tradition was revived by a group of local people, led by shopkeeper Jean George, in the mid-1980s and is now combined with **Gloucester Day**, which celebrates the lifting of the Siege.

Charles II Statue

The War of the Elvers

In the 1870s a dispute arose, called the **'Elver Wars'**, about elvering from the River Severn. Gloucester had become an industrial city with a much-increased population and what had previously been small-scale elvering became a major operation on the Lower Severn. This meant there was a much-depleted stock of elvers (or baby eels) to migrate further upstream to places like Tewkesbury, Upton-on-Severn and Worcester. The newly-formed Severn Fisheries Board banned elvering and a law was passed in 1874 which made it illegal to take elvers from the Lower Severn. An inquiry in 1876 led to elvering being allowed once more.

Elvers, although not widely-eaten in this country, are seen as a delicacy in Japan.

OBJECTS

The Prehistoric Mirror and the World's Oldest Backgammon Set are Displayed Here.

The Museum of Gloucester has an enormous collection of artefacts but two of the most important are the Birdlip Mirror - **the largest prehistoric bronze mirror ever found** - and the Gloucester Tables Set, which is **the oldest complete backgammon set in the world!**

The mysterious mirror was discovered accidently in the summer of 1879 by a road mender called Joseph Barnfield in Birdlip. It is one of only 60 found in the world and, based on its appearance, belonged to a wealthy owner.

The Gloucester Tables Set is the earliest surviving board and complete set of counters for the game tabula, a predecessor of backgammon. Dating from the 11th or early 12th century, it is an example of Romanesque art. It was discovered on the site of Gloucester Castle in 1983.

The Birdlip Mirror

The UK's Oldest Post Box was Made Here

The **oldest working pillar box in UK** can be found at Barnes Cross, near Sherborne in Dorset. The octagonal box was manufactured by John M Butt & Company of Gloucester in **1853**, just a year after roadside pillar boxes were first introduced. It has a vertical letter aperture which officials originally thought would prove harder to steal from.

Gloucester has its Own Tart!

In Gloucester, a tart similar to a Bakewell Tart was made using ground rice, raspberry jam and almond essence. In May 2013, council leader **Paul James** discovered a recipe for **"Gloucester Tart"** in a Gloucester history book. Subsequently, Gloucester museums revived the recipe, serving complimentary Gloucester Tarts to museum patrons.

BUSINESS

The Multi-Million Pound Internet Company Founded in a Gloucester Bedroom

Web hosting company Fasthosts was founded in 1999 by 17 year-old Andrew Michael in his bedroom in Abbeydale as part of an A level project. He sold the company for **£61 million** to United Internet in 2006. Fasthosts' Christmas parties had become legendary with stars like Girls Aloud and the Sugababes performing.

The First British Jet-Engined Aircraft

The Gloster E28/39, designed and built by the Gloster Aircraft Company and powered by engineer and pilot **Frank Whittle's jet engine**, was the first British jet-engined aircraft. It was designed to test the Whittle jet engine in flight, leading to the development of the Gloster Meteor. Its official first flight was at RAF Cranwell on 15 May 1941, but it had already left the ground during taxiing trials at Gloster's Brockworth airfield on 8 April. A full-size fibreglass model of the aircraft can be seen at the Jet Age Museum at Staverton.

Whittle was only 21 when he first presented the idea of turbo-jet propulsion to his bosses at the Air Ministry. They showed no interest so he patented it himself in 1932, but it lapsed as he couldn't afford to renew it. Only years later did his idea become reality.

A Match Made in Gloucester

Match-making company, **S. J. Moreland and Sons**, was established on the outskirts of Gloucester in 1867, and went on to produce the iconic **England's Glory** matches - and although the brand went bust in the 70s, a pub of the same name still exists on London Road. A lighting feature of the England's Glory logo is still in place on the company's former factory on Bristol Road, which closed in 1976 and is now a trading estate for small businesses. In 2014 upmarket designer Anya Hindmarch produced a clutch bag using the England's Glory logo (price £1295!), which **Harry Potter star Emma Watson** was seen using on a night out at the British Fashion Awards.

The former Moreland's Match Factory

007's Shirts are Made Here

Emma Willis, a boutique **bespoke shirtmaker** located on the famous Jermyn Street in London, manufactures her shirts at the historic Bearland House in Longsmith Street, Gloucester. Celebrity clients include **Prince Charles, Benedict Cumberbatch, Colin Firth and 007 Daniel Craig.**

Gloucester Cattle Saved from Extinction

Gloucester Cattle are one of the oldest breeds of dairy cattle, dating back to the 13th century. By 1972 only one significant herd remained **and the breed was in danger of dying out**. The Gloucester Cattle Society was revived in 1973 and the breed has moved from near extinction to being rated by the Rare Breeds Survival Trust as being "At Risk", as there are still fewer than 750 registered breeding females. In 2021, the RBST said herd numbers had further halved between 2006 and 2020 due to fewer farmers breeding them, with only 26 herds as of April 2021.

The milk of Gloucester Cattle is well-suited to cheese-making, being high in protein and with high butterfat. **Single Gloucester** and **Stinking Bishop** cheeses are made exclusively from Gloucester Cattle's milk.

The Pig That Saved the City

The Gloucester Old Spot is said to be the largest pig ever to be bred. They graze in apple orchards and the large black spots on their white give rise to the legend that they are bruises from falling apples. By legend, it is **the pig that "saved the city"** during the **Siege of Gloucester** by making so much noise that the **Royalists thought there were lots of pigs** and there was no danger of the Parliamentarians running out of food!

They became the first breed of any species in the world to be given Traditional Speciality Guaranteed status by the EU Commission putting it on a par with Champagne and Parma ham. The Old Spot was the subject of the "**Henson Pig Trail**" in 2017, named after farmer **Joe Henson**, the saviour of many rare breeds, founder of Cotswold Farm Park and father of television presenter **Adam Henson.**

Olbas Oil is Manufactured Here

Olbas Oil, the well-known decongestant relief, is manufactured by **G R Lane Health Products** in Sisson Road, Gloucester.

The Biggest Ice Cream Factory in Europe

Gloucester's **Walls Ice Cream** factory (now Unilever) was once the largest in all of Europe. It was built in 1959, and the factory underwent a major expansion in 1981 when Unilever merged all ice-cream production in Gloucester with the shutting down of its factory in Acton, London. Walls initially were a meat producer and **Walls sausages** were one of its well-known brands. In 1922, the sales were falling in the summer season, so to avoid layings-off in their workforce, they began to manufacture ice cream, and that is how it came to expand. In 2021, the factory was forecast to produce **145 million litres of ice cream.**

The Gloucester Motorcycle Which Won the Isle of Man TT Race

The **Cotton Motor Company**, a motorcycle manufacturer, was founded in Gloucester by Frank Willoughby Cotton in 1918. In 1923, **Stanley Woods won the Isle of Man TT riding a Cotton machine.** This generated orders allowing a move to new premises in Quay Street. The factory moved to Stratton Road in 1970, then to Bolton in 1978, closing in 1980.

The Gloucester-Made Toys that Travelled the World

Roberts Brothers made toys and games from the 1890s at the **Glevum Works on Upton Street** and were once considered to be the UK's largest maker of toys and games, at one point employing more than 750 people. The firm developed from a simple party game Piladex, devised by brothers Harry Owen Roberta and John Owen Roberts for a Sunday school class.

The range of their products was immense, and they were exported across the world. The most common items were games, with **ludo, snakes and ladders and dominoes** amongst their greatest production. They also made dolls and soft toys and patented what was the first version of a game which became known as **Subbuteo**. They were taken over by another toy company, **Chad Valley**, and then closed down in 1956.

The Largest Pin-Making Centre in the World

It is estimated that there were more than one hundred small domestic pin suppliers in England around 1760, mostly around the city of Gloucester. By 1735 pin making was "the chief manufacture of the city".

It was probably the largest pin-making centre in Britain (and probably the World) by 1763, employing 1,200 men, women and children. The building which is currently 'The Folk of Gloucester' in Westgate Street was a pin factory as was what is now the Irish Club in Horton Road.

The bollards in the pedestrianised gate streets are believed to be based on Gloucester's pin-making history.

A sample Bollard based on an ornate pin

SPORT

Gloucester Rugby Didn't Always Play in Cherry & White

The **Cherry and Whites**, as they are now known, were called by different names over the years, including "**The Elver Eaters**". They didn't always play in cherry and white either. According to local legend, at the Gloucester Club's first meeting it was decided that the Club's uniform was to be **entirely navy blue**. Yet on an away trip they realised they had forgotten to bring sufficient navy strip for the entire team, leaving behind a kit bag full of shirts. Travelling en route through **Painswick**, they stopped off at the local rugby club and asked to borrow a strip for the game. **Painswick RFC loaned them 15 of their cherry and white jerseys**. The Gloucester side went on to win the away fixture and **failed to return the shirts** to Painswick, adopting the colours as their own.

On Track for a World Record

On 10.00am on Saturday 2nd May 1982 a remarkable 24-hour track race started on the Blackbridge Athletics Track in Podsmead, Gloucester. Organised by Gloucester Athletic Club, a number of record performances were set including a stunning new **World Record for 24 hours of 170 miles 974 yards (274.480 kms) set by club member Dave Dowdle.**

The Boxer Unbeaten for a Decade

Gloucester-born lightweight boxer **Hal Bagwell** (1918-2001) retained to the end his British record of being **unbeaten in the ring for more than 10 years**. The claim, made on his behalf in the **Guinness Book of Records**, attributed to him the world record for the most consecutive professional boxing contests without a loss (an amazing 183 consecutive fights between August 10, 1938, and November 29, 1948) although he himself repudiated that, saying the number was nearer 83.

The Rugby World Cup and Celebrity Masterchef Winner

Gloucester, England and British Lions rugby star is not only a **World Cup Winner** (in 2003), but he also triumphed in **Celebrity Masterchef** (in 2011). This created the potential for some confusion, as there is already a celebrity chef called **Phil Vickery**, who appeared on the "This Morning" programme and was married to Fern Britton. Our Phil was appointed a Deputy Lieutenant of Gloucestershire in 2015.

ENTERTAINMENT

The Film Peter Rabbit 2 was Partly Set in Gloucester

The film **Peter Rabbit 2,** released in 2021, has some of its plot based around a **Farmers Market in Gloucester**. One scene shows a shot of the **Docks with the Cathedral in the background** and **the House of the Tailor of Gloucester** in College Court, with some computer-generated alterations, is shown several times. The Farmers Market in the film takes place in a Square on a Saturday, whereas the real Gloucester Farmers Market is held on The Cross on Fridays.

The Beatles Played at The Regal

In March 1963, a little-known band called **The Beatles** played at **The Regal theatre in King's Square** (now a Wetherspoon's pub) as **a support act for American singers Tommy Roe and Chris Montez.** Citizen journalist **Hugh Worsnip** was sent to the New County Hotel after the performance to interview Montez and ended up meeting The Beatles. He asked them to write their names in his reporter's notebook so he would get the spelling correct, but threw the book away just before they hit the big time!

The Tailor of Gloucester was Based on a Real-Life Incident

The Tailor of Gloucester is a children's book written and illustrated by **Beatrix Potter**, privately printed by the author in 1902, and published in a trade edition **by Frederick Warne & Co**. in October 1903. For years, Potter declared that of all her books it was her personal favourite. **The tale was based on a real-world incident involving John Prichard** (1877 - 1934), a Gloucester tailor commissioned to make a waistcoat for the new mayor. He returned to his shop on a Monday morning to find the waistcoat almost completed. A note attached read, "No more twist". **His assistants had worked on the waistcoat in the night**, but Prichard encouraged a fiction that **fairies had done the work** and the incident became a local legend. **The Tailor's shop was in Westgate Street** (part of what is now The Sword Inn) but Potter preferred the look of a nearby property in College Court, which she sketched instead. Today this continues as the **"House of the Tailor of Gloucester"** shop and attraction.

The House of the Tailor of Gloucester

Our Own X-Factor Winner (in China!)

Gloucester-born singer **Mary-Jess Leaverland**, who attended St Peter's High School, won **Min Xing Chang Fan Tian** (or in English: I Want to Sing to the Stars), **the Chinese version of the X Factor**, which was televised to 70 million people in December 2009. She also sang the theme tune for Downton Abbey, had one of her songs included on the Rugby World Cup 2011 album and sang **'Abide With Me'** before the 2012 FA Cup Final.

Dickens Performs in Westgate Street

32-34 Westgate Street (the former Poundstretcher store) is located on the site of the former Theatre Royal, built in 1791 by John Boles Watson. The Theatre Royal was the former centre of culture in Gloucester, and once had **Charles Dickens** perform the trial scene from The Pickwick Papers to a capacity audience.

Gloucester Leisure Centre Hosted Big Name Acts

Gloucester Leisure Centre played host to lots of big name music acts from 1976, including **Bucks Fizz, Cliff Richard, Culture Club, Duran Duran, Englebert Humperdinck, Gene Pitney, Johnny Mathis, Madness, The Nolans, Shakin Stevens, Status Quo, Tina Turner and Van Morrison.**

Dalek School Rumour Exterminated

The Christmas special episode of **Dr Who**, featuring **David Tennant** as The Doctor, was filmed in Gloucester in 2008. A second episode was recorded in 2019, with Jodie Whittaker in the lead role. However, rumours that **an architectural feature on Denmark Road High School** inspired the Dalek character are said not to be true.

Denmark Road High School

Austin Powers Inspiration Caught in the Act

Peter Wyngarde, the actor whose detective character **Jason King** is said to have **inspired Austin Powers**, was fined for an act of **'gross indecency'** in the **Gloucester bus station toilets** in 1975.

Cheese Rolling Could be Over 600 Years Old

The first written evidence of **cheese rolling** is found from a message written to the Gloucester town crier in 1826; even then it was apparent the event was an old tradition, and is believed to be **at least six hundred years old**. Some say it was all about claiming grazing rights on the common and land around Cooper's Hill, others believe it could have been a fertility ritual. **The 7.5lb cheese** can reach **speeds of up to 70mph on the 1 in 2 gradient Cooper's Hill,** taking approximately 12 seconds to get from top to bottom. Videos of the cheese rolling have been watched literally millions of times on YouTube.

Paw Patrol's UK Voices Were Recorded Here

The **voices for the UK version** of US-made children's programme **Paw Patrol** were dubbed by a company based in Churcham, just outside Gloucester. A number of local schoolchildren provided the voices, including Crypt School pupil **Fraser Martin** who played the character **Tracker**. Fraser was also the UK voice of **Frankie Fritz** in **'Rusty Rivets'** on **Nickelodeon**. He **also played the Boy King** in the re-enactment of **Henry III's coronation** at Gloucester Cathedral in 2016.

Cliff's Guitarist Recorded a Single in Gloucester Prison (He was only visiting!)

Jet Harris was the bass guitarist in **Cliff Richard's** backing group. It was originally called **The Drifters** but renamed **The Shadows** following the threat of litigation from the US band of the same name. He left The Shadows in 1962 and released a series of solo records. In 1977 he gave a performance in **Gloucester Prison's chapel** which was recorded and released on vinyl. Jet lived in Gloucester for a number of years.

Gloucester is a Popular Filming Location

The old warehouses at Gloucester have provided ideal backgrounds for shooting scenes for period television dramas and feature films, including the **Onedin Line and Vanity Fair**. Five tall ships, including Irene, Kathleen & May and Earl of Pembroke, gathered at Gloucester to take part in filming scenes for Disney's **'Through the Looking Glass'** on 18 Aug 2014. The main action took place on the quay beside the Waterways Museum, but props were distributed around both sides of the docks, and the film crew 'dressed' the adjoining buildings to hide all traces of modernity.

Gloucester's historic cathedral cloisters were transformed into the corridors of **Hogwart's School of Witchcraft and Wizardry** in the films of JK Rowling's first two books - **Harry Potter and the Philosopher's Stone and Harry Potter and the Chamber of Secrets**. All modern signs, locks and electrics had to be disguised under panels painted to look like the stone walls. One such fitting remains there today, covering a light switch, and will be forever known as 'the Harry Potter box'.

Gloucester has been part of the film set for many movies. One of the lesser-known ones is **'Outlaw'** released in 2007. One of the scenes was filmed with stars **Sean Bean and Danny Dyer** inside a white transit van parked at the Land Registry car park off Station Road.

MILITARY CONNECTIONS

There Have Been 10 HMS Gloucesters

There have been **10 HMS Gloucester ships**, with the final one being retired from service in 2011. The bell from **one of the ships is hung in the Council Chamber at North Warehouse** in Gloucester Docks and **another is on display in the Museum of Gloucester**. The 9th HMS Gloucester was sunk during the German invasion of Crete during the Second World War.

A bell from one of HMS Gloucester on display
at Gloucester Museum

The Glosters Were the Only Regiment with a Back Badge

On 21 March, during the Battle of Alexandria, French cavalry broke through the British lines, formed up behind the regiment, and began to charge. With the men still heavily engaged to their front, **the order was given for the rear rank to turn about**, and standing thus in two ranks **back-to-back**, the regiment held the line.

To commemorate this action, the regiment began wearing a **badge on the back** as well as the front of the headdress, **a unique distinction in the British Army** that was officially sanctioned in 1830. The Gloucestershire Regiment inherited from the 28th Regiment the privilege of wearing the back badge. It was a privilege that the 2nd Battalion did not want, but it was made palatable to the former 61st Regiment by replacing the number 28 with the Sphinx, a battle honour awarded to both predecessor regiments.

<u>War Hero Colonel's Carved Cross</u>

Colonel James Carne led 837 men of the Gloucester-shire Regiment against more than 27,000 Chinese in the Battle of Imjin River for three days in April 1951, on what has now become known as Gloster Hill.

Colonel Carne was eventually captured by Communist forces and spent 19 months in solitary confinement. He was later **awarded the Victoria Cross.** During his time in captivity, he carved a Celtic cross out of volcanic rock using, it is believed, just a nail. **The cross is now on display in Gloucester Cathedral. Colonel Carne's Victoria Cross is displayed in the Soldiers of Gloucestershire Museum in Gloucester Docks.**

GLOUCESTER AROUND THE WORLD

$5 Million Korean Battle Monument

During the Korean War the **Gloucestershire Regiment of 837** defended **Hill 235 (now known as Gloster Hill)** against the North Korean and Chinese offensive **of 27,000 for three days despite being outnumbered 32-1**. They fought until they ran out of ammunition; **217 were captured and 620 killed compared to estimates of 10-15,000 Chinese.** Their sacrifice held the Chinese offensive up long enough for the United Nations to regroup and launch a counter offensive and push them back. Without the Glosters' heroic stand at the Battle of Imjin River it is likely there would not be a South Korea at all. The South Koreans in recognition of this have created several memorials and monuments to commemorate The Glosters. During the whole Korean War only 3 Victoria Crosses were awarded - 2 of them were awarded at the Battle of Imjin River.

The Gloucester Valley Battle Monument or **Gloucester Memorial** is a memorial in South Korea that commemorates the actions of the Gloucestershire Regiment and C Troop, 170th Mortar Battery, Royal Artillery, of the British Army during the **Battle of the Imjin River** in 1951. The memorial was first unveiled on 29 June 1957. The memorial park was expanded and reopened in 2014.

There is a memorial garden on the east side of the

stream containing **a large sculpture of the Glosters' beret, a set of life-sized Gloster soldiers patrolling away from the Imjin River** and a memorial wall. The stream is crossed by **"The Heroes of Gloucester Bridge"** and a path leads round to a flight of steps that takes you to the memorial stones set into a wall built into the side of the hill.

The Oldest Bells in the USA

The **oldest set of bells in the USA** are in Old North Church, Boston. Made in 1744 by the **Rudhall foundry in Gloucester**, they were installed in 1745. The bells were transported free from Gloucester because they were very good ballast. **Paul Revere** was **a bell ringer at the church** and made the historic ride to warn American troops that "**The British are coming**" during the War of Independence. Rudhall's foundry was on the site of the Post Office in King's Square. Two Rudhall bells from 1710 are on display in St Michael's Tower at the Cross.

The Organist's Son Who Wrote the Music to the US National Anthem

Born in Gloucester in 1750, the son of the Gloucester Cathedral organist, former King's School student **John Stafford** Smith wrote the music for "The Anacreontic Song" which became America's National Anthem, known as **"The Star-Spangled Banner"** in 1931. A memorial for him can now be found in Gloucester Cathedral.

Memorial Plaque to John Stafford Smith

POLITICS AND CIVIC LIFE

Gloucester was Blair's Top Target

As Leader of the Opposition, **Tony Blair targeted Gloucester as the seat he needed to win** to gain a majority in Parliament in the 1997 general election. He launched Labour's campaign in the city and his spin doctor **Peter (now Lord) Mandelson** was said to use images of Gloucester Cathedral on presentations he gave about election planning. It worked - Labour gained the seat with a majority of over 8,000 and won a landslide victory giving them a 179-seat majority in Parliament.

Gloucester's Multi-Lingual MP

Gloucester MP Richard Graham has lived and worked in ten countries and **speaks eight languages**: Indonesian, Cantonese, Mandarin, Tagalog, French, Malay, Swahili and English. Graham **was the first MP to speak Indonesian in the Chamber**, when he spoke during Prime Minister's Questions on 10 October 2018 on the natural disaster at Palu in Indonesia's Sulawesi islands.

The Mayor's Chain and the Year-Long Debate on Horseshoes!

The **Mayor of Gloucester's chain and badge of office are made of 18-carat gold**, the form being a double row of a hundred horse-shoe links. The Mayor's chain and badge were purchased by subscription at a cost of £220 and presented to the Corporation in April 1870. In 1932/3 the mayor of the day, W.L. Edwards, had the horseshoes reversed. They had been mounted with their points downwards, and he had them replaced points upwards. This reflects the modern idea that the luck of horseshoes is trapped within the bowl formed by the bow of the shoe. Theodore Hannam-Clarke became mayor for 1933/4 and remembered the chain as his father had worn it - with the shoes pointing down. After a year-long debate, which attracted national media attention, and the discovery that there had been no council approval for the action, the chain was restored to its original form!

Gloucester's Two Coats of Arms

The **City of Gloucester** actually **has two coats of arms**. **The first, (The Tudor Arms)** granted in 1538 by Henry VIII, is little-used now. On the Tudor coat, **the roses** appear to refer to those of Lancaster and York, **the boar's head** to the badge of Richard, Duke of Gloucester, afterwards King Richard III, who granted the Town its Charter of Incorporation in 1483. **The horseshoes and nails** are symbolic of the early trade of Gloucester which in the twelfth century, and probably before, was famous for its ironworks and smithery.

The second (the Commonwealth Arms), introduced in 1652, includes a motto **"Fides invicta triumphat" (Unconquered faith triumphs).** These represent **the siege the city withstood in the Civil War.** These new arms were actually declared void by Charles II but the city ignored him and in 1945 the full achievement was confirmed by the College of Heralds.

Who's Got the Sheriff? (We Have!)

Gloucester is **one of only 15 towns and cities** in England and Wales to **retain the ancient office of Sheriff.** The Sheriff's office dates back to the 1200s and is a far older position than the Mayor. The National Association of City and Town Sheriffs of England and Wales was founded in Gloucester in 1984 by the then Sheriff Councillor Andrew Gravells.

Parliament was Held in Gloucester

Many significant **parliaments were held at Gloucester** over the centuries including one held by Henry IV in 1407 which paved the way for **bringing public finances under parliamentary control.**

RELIGION

The Sunday School Founder

Philanthropist **Robert Raikes**, the pioneer of **Sunday Schools**, was born in Gloucester in 1736, and was baptised in the city at **St Mary de Crypt** Church. Famed for his contribution to the promotion of Sunday Schools in 1780, Robert used his paper, the Gloucester Journal, which he took over from his father, for publicity, with several schools opening in and around Gloucester across two years. **A statue of him was erected in Gloucester Park** in 1930, **which is a copy of one erected on London's Victoria Embankment** 50 years earlier.

Robert Raikes House, where the Sunday School Founder lived

The Bishop Burnt at the Stake

John Hooper (1495-1555), Bishop of Gloucester, was **burnt at the stake for heresy** during the reign of Queen Mary I. He was a proponent of the English Reformation when the Church of England broke away from the authority of the Pope and the Roman Catholic Church.

When Queen Mary I ascended to the throne in 1553, it doomed John as Mary was a Catholic Queen. The execution took place in St Mary's Square, near the Cathedral, where a monument to him now stands. The Folk of Gloucester in Westgate Street has what is claimed to be part of the stake.

Bishop Hooper's Monument in St Mary's Square

The Preacher Who Captivated America

George Whitefield, who was born at the **Bell Inn in Southgate Street** and attended **The Crypt School,** was an Anglican cleric and evangelist who was **one of the founders of Methodism and the evangelical movement.**

In 1740, Whitefield **travelled to North America,** where he preached a series of revivals that became part of the "Great Awakening". He preached at least 18,000 times to perhaps **10 million listeners in Great Britain and her American colonies.** Whitefield preached his first sermon at **St Mary de Crypt Church** in Southgate Street and **the pulpit in which he stood is still there today.**

The Signature Tune of the WI

Jerusalem, the signature tune of the **Women's Institute,** was written by **Hubert Parry** (1848 - 1918). He spent his childhood years at the family home of **Highnam Court,** a mile or two over the Severn from the city, within sight of the Cathedral. Originally composed for chorus and organ, Parry wrapped his rousing tune around the words of a poem by **William Blake.**

COMMUNITY

The Area with over 70 Languages

Over 70 languages are spoken in the **Barton area**, making it one of the most diverse places in the country.

ROYAL CONNECTIONS

Our Very Own Duke Became King

The title of **Duke of Gloucester** was created in 1385. It was initially seen as an unlucky title as its first three holders did not produce an heir. It died out for over 150 years when its most famous holder **acceded to the throne as Richard III** in 1483. It didn't exist again until 1659 when it was awarded to Henry Stuart, son of King Charles I.

The current holder of the Dukedom, **Prince Richard**, inherited the title in 1974 on the death of his father. He had become heir apparent when his elder brother Prince William died in 1972 when his plane crashed in a flying competition.

Alfred the Great's Mint

A mint was created in Gloucester by Alfred The Great in 871, issuing silver pennies. . A mint remained in the city until the end of the reign of Henry III in 1272, signifying the importance of Gloucester. The Domesday Book reports that King William drew £20 as an annual rent from the mint.

The Pie Fit for a King (Or Queen)

From medieval times to 1836 it was customary for Gloucester to **send a lamprey pie to the monarch every Christmas**.

After 1836 expense brought an end to the annual custom, and these days **the lamprey** is an endangered species. But for special occasions - coronations, jubilees and so on - **Gloucester still sends a Royal Lamprey Pie to the King or Queen - Queen Elizabeth II** was provided with one for her Coronation, her Silver Jubilee in 1977, the Golden Jubilee in 2002, the Diamond Jubilee in 2012 and when Her Majesty became the longest-reigning Monarch in 2015.

King Henry I (1068-1135) is said to have died from eating too many Lampreys ; although most historians believe he may have died from food poisoning.

Printed by Amazon Italia Logistica S.r.l.
Torrazza Piemonte (TO), Italy

28329041R00058